punishment bag

Mary Burritt Christiansen Poetry Series

Mary Burritt Christiansen Poetry Series

HILDA RAZ, *Series Editor*

The Mary Burritt Christiansen Poetry Series publishes two to four books a year that engage and give voice to the realities of living, working, and experiencing the West and the Border as places and as metaphors. The purpose of the series is to expand access to, and the audience for, quality poetry, both single volumes and anthologies, that can be used for general reading as well as in classrooms.

Also available in the Mary Burritt Christiansen Poetry Series:

Midsummer Count: New and Selected Poems by Robin Becker
a chronology of blood: poems by Teo Shannon
small lives: poems by Gary Jackson
A Real Man Would Have a Gun: Poems by Stacey Waite
Dream of the Bird Tattoo: Poems and Sueñitos by Juan J. Morales
Unruly Tree: Poems by Leslie Ullman
A Walk with Frank O'Hara: Poems by Susan Aizenberg
Light of Wings: Poems by Sarah Kotchian
Trials and Tribulations of Dirty Shame, Oklahoma: And Other Prose Poems by Sy Hoahwah
A Guide to Tongue Tie Surgery: Poems by Tina Carlson

For additional titles in the Mary Burritt Christiansen Poetry Series, please visit unmpress.com.

Punishment

Jake

Bag

Fournier

Poems

ALBUQUERQUE
UNIVERSITY OF NEW MEXICO PRESS

Printed in the United States of America

Library of Congress Cataloging-in-Publication Data

Names: Fournier, Jake, 1989– author

Title: Punishment bag / [Jake Fournier].

Other titles: Punishment bag (Compilation) | Mary Burritt Christiansen poetry series

Description: [Albuquerque] : [University of New Mexico Press], [2026] | Series: Mary Burritt Christiansen poetry series

Identifiers: LCCN 2025035318 |
ISBN 9780826369222 paperback |
ISBN 9780826369239 epub

Subjects: LCGFT: Poetry

Classification: LCC PS3606.O8445 P86 2026

LC record available at https://lccn.loc.gov/2025035318

Founded in 1889, the University of New Mexico sits on the traditional homelands of the Pueblo of Sandia. The original peoples of New Mexico—Pueblo, Navajo, and Apache—since time immemorial have deep connections to the land and have made significant contributions to the broader community statewide. We honor the land itself and those who remain stewards of this land throughout the generations and also acknowledge our committed relationship to Indigenous peoples. We gratefully recognize our history.

Cover illustration by Isaac Morris
Designed by Isaac Morris
Composed in Cormerant Garamond

for my mother, Joanne

Contents

Contents

Your Friends...Poets

I

Your Friends . . . Poets

Natural Piety

These rainbows don't bend,
    aren't light, though they are delightful.
Distorted in an hourglass
    I found them here amid my papers.

I love rooms filled with paper—
    half the paper should be overcovered
and the other half, woven canvas,
    denim cardboard—white in the sense
it isn't tempered, some call
it stone, others wheat or fiber.

And now that we're here in this room together
you see that the rainbeams I mean are internal.

Beams in that they do not bend,
    rain in that they are refractal,
they marked once a promise between us and heaven
then the excision that the eye is good for
    from a spectrum where the invisible
    pops both ends, like a spriteful child.

And so with things we can't see
    is it thus ever: we lend them
    the name of the nearest behavior.

Quick Recovery

I put on my thigh-highs and
    step into the gulch.
The slicked rocks strewn
    with exploded carp
and plastic garbage
    give way gradually to
the sulfurous waters where
    they say the boy drowned.
My arms in
    to the shoulder,
I turn my face up to a sky
    so bright its blue
oozes around the outline of
    a crooked pine. Nineteen
and a half and high, he'd
    been a toiler in the pit one
summer and this was
    unemployed. I know
a little about work so my
    sympathy is right where
you'd expect it to lie. If his gut
    didn't split he'd have
floated to the surface, but
    his face is calm enough that
when they get him drained
    if they still want to
they'll open the casket at
    the chapel. I never had beef
with ugliness, can hardly
    get drunk, don't go in

much for Jesus, but
    I know He said, "I'll make
you fishers of men," and a
    couple other things that
in my case proved true. For godsake
    if you want to get from
here to happiness you go straight
    through. You dig like
I tell my kids all the way to
    China. Showering at the station
though I'm trying to picture
    it right and seems like you'd
come up somewhere in
    the ocean, or on some
Pacific island, maybe
    Indonesia.

Happiness

The three of us drink sparkling water.
Slanted so that the kitchen table bears
all its weight on two legs, the floor
gleams in blue daylight.

"This is what I was talking about,"
you say, holding up a funny orange.

There is no end to what we share, and yet we don't
share everything. The fruit
basket, itself the fruit in its own
shadow, soaks up advertisements for charity from the radio,
and a quick laugh externalizes us to each other;

each of us is neither. You play a symbiote
in the gentle insistence, sure, but inside
it, separating, you think—if I could be one
of them, I'd be the lighter
one, and like me you'd

fill the situation until, easy
to like, lovely, with no one
pained, nothing remembered, a split'd form
in ownership and address, and

you'd make a you of yourself again. Then,

not knowing a word, you'll look up
what possession does,
and like a glass blower coloring

a bubble, your brainstem
will suck in more than the signals
it receives until the character
it gives back in motor function and your limbs'
accomplishments is infused with giant
concepts, deep wells
of intelligence. Both the kind that
readjusts the chair and the kind
that stands on it. Get up there and see

Your Release

The day of your release we ate gorditas
in the Kmart plaza—whatever ties had been between us
were caducous, I felt, watching women,
their hair destroyed by chemicals and wiry,
hunch over their steering wheels, frantic at their scratch-offs.
If one you loved in life and lost comes back
from the dead trailing plutonic phosphorescence,
a widow to his living self, mourning what he might have lived,
cups his viduity beneath his eyes and turns to thank you,
would you have the heart to look in them and ask
what it was like?
I did.

The sky was clearish urine colored, blue clouds to the south.
Your mother was fine—you'd get back to her properties
and clean whatever needed to be cleaned,
clear brush and weed. I said it might not feel good now,
but if you lived say ten years right . . .

Firefield 5 × 50

A McDonald's on our left a mile back switches
sides when the highway bends.
Too tired tonight to do anything but drive, we set out for . . .
You're saying something about your life,
How easy,
And not until we've passed does the girl
streak—her soaked
hair caked, Or shirt-pattern—Her feet are
She's running on, The light, A girl made out,
But not Annie.
We almost forget she crossed.
A disconnected gloriole follows the drive, and the drive
draws out of us,
Thick and ribbon-like, two latencies, Avoided ever since.
Because their significance and their insignificance
coincide. And it's midnight, Just about.
Your leg tapers like a tine, Like a horn
into the gas, and I see how.

Waiting on Ed (A Bachelor Party)

I sit down at a table full of men.
Okay then.
I don't want to be who I am.

This belongs to a special category of thought.

Where, iridescing like gills,
the apertures that determine us
give to or refuse the plasm of what happened—
          shame, sound, a new

     being—the eggs of us hatch these.

At the back entrances, staff are talking.
          They said they would see.
     We open little paper-covered cups
with imaginary causes. Our speech in long orbits
since we are no longer friends
                                        or strangers
once or twice approaches
near enough to our beliefs.

Your Property

You can't tell this *A* from an *uh.*
Then consequence builds its spine:
a trunk. One you know better
in your shoulder than to sight.
Like a serif on an implied line
shaping a gravity that, because existing
only in us, it can't bear, your stuff
soon accumulates inside.
As each pearl nods to another gem
you move there. Quick aleph
in alfalfa, in that
field you've not once forgotten
you own, your brain
sporadically fits an extra acre.

Fresh Lettuce

between blue and yellow
in indifference

a detached sense
draws me without self

not selfless—what I couldn't help
under care or neglected

is what I would help
in you

both primaries
tuck into my head

a head of living paper
and then these folds warp

into your interior clothes, a dress
whose materials give what they are

their power
if that is the word for this

force, this force that
moves through us

like a sickle
even as we stand not talking

together, then we'll be more
attentive in the future

Garden-Level

Remember, you are freeing yourself.
    This mentor, reimagined as an X-ray,
    makes a flat strip of your jaw.
A clump of asparagus grows under vigilance.
Dark-green florets interrupt.
Its livid stems. The fuchsia smells.
Now spin it in an orb, she says, until you have
a floating earthen ball, vegetal isomorph
of the Dog Star bursting with Françoise
    spears: that's one link.
    But how it threads—
    explode how you will—
    is before will,
and could we go back you would stay here.

Canadian Schoolboy

Magnetic north—
you have imagination of a sort.

Enough to make compromises.

And if you did
whatever you wanted?

You'd shoe this expedition with a size—

tin and nitrous, rations—these
to distinguish it from the diagnosis

that the diagnosis is. That is

to say that the distance crossed
is not a cross, but two sticks

lengthwise, in tandem, the one laid

after the other one meter
at a time, the two each time almost touching

but never quite.

M.

That's just the way this bird flies, tagged
at the heel, caught, caught
dead.
In your account, a bunch once alive
jams a link. Chain-link the handsaw's
cold orphrey.
How sad,
I said, gross facsimiles of people turned
clockwise
while on another platform inappropriate
feelings made me misguide
someone. The most generous
narcissism, reverse of unconscious righteousness,
would have me publicize my internal
conflict over M.'s excessive ego.
Ego ergo ego.
A swan's head is just the end of its neck,
but a dove's wings steeple.

Livable City

So many ways can be head on.
It is what it is, but still-uncertain
Iditaroders all after a grebe,
inward Alaska, ride
customized Treks into Columbus's DUMBO
more than to remind us of rust.
There's rust, and now its shadow in the rain,
but it's a mistake, and it's a mistake to say
you cared
or, "But I really care." An igneous nail
in being exactly what you seem—silver-watched &
salmon-chinoed—what you saw in yesterday's ad
is here. You couldn't unseem it.
Who arbitrates what constitutes harm?
His meat, crisp like chestnut's,
replaces your germ.

Woodland Pattern

Walking by the river in Milwaukee,
honey-dark with industrial runoff,
you, and you and me,
connect over pre-Cambrian fossils
you've been collecting
near Coralville. For most
of my life I've been shifting a few hours
to the left or right along I-80/90.
New Mexico will be different.
There, fentanyl and lost retirees
shake up to the top. The sky thins.
Quietly a daughter walks her father to a fishing hole.
Then we're left to the sound
of walking along the river in Milwaukee.
When we come up from the ravine,
you manage to make friends
with the bookstore clerks while you
browse alone in the other room, and I wander
back and forth between the two of you.
Why is it important that you're both you?
Close-up, equality confuses us,
but a certain love insists on it
such as the three of us feel
instinctively for Milwaukee,
a city that only sifts the greater will-lessness
that repossesses everything eventually
and where, in perfect stillness, we are living
tomorrow, watching the current
erase itself after the last waters
fall away across the surface.

Friendship

One of the two outlets doesn't work,
            didn't—
and the rope. "I killed that . . ." and smoke—
    all around us is smoke, sunlight—your salt.
On the stairs urging you into disinterest
            so that, disinterested,
a hypocrite in full knowledge,
just incapable, with your back like particle board
under my hand, I, out of body, see a fraudulent
comforter.

It burns when we withdraw.
        So I touch me,
tardily—
it passes for suffering.

Should we name the source proximity we'd be too close.

Dreyman

The gray-scale blowup
    the pistil draws above
a repeated evening: whistling boy
    with jawline
off. He loves her yet the pain.
    One must not do good wrong,
they say. Hull and
    as it jerks with the 16-bit
soundtrack, it's afternoon
    again, only this time really drenched in it
they run the generator and
    watch him. Thank God
for those games without
    which, though drawn beside
repeatedly, any
    progress is a feeling.

Lessons from Three Paws

To breathe life back into, as I'm told
this bull did—well, I've seen the same
after a rescue. True inspiration.
"He won't last the night," and I don't go here
because it's the exception but because, last night
as your chest rose, your ribs were clearly fingers.

In a coextensive plain, a mop
rots into its head. Now here,
undoubtedly, was once a scene of really
extraordinary violence.

Be present—
it came from every angle, and is
still probably coming, fresh for some, from some
as if unfolding in time were a savior.

What's the danger?

At the center of every life
is a partition with something on the other side.

A Kitchen in the 19ième

«C'est un plaisir d'aider nos amis»—
this response I wanted in the kitchen
of a colocation in the 19th in the spring of 2016
came to me just now on a sheetrock hillside
in the Otero Canyon. A zebraman
named Wilfrid, gray-haired, athletic
little smoker who had his bike and various
accessories zebra striped to suit his quirk,
would hassle me in speedy French
about my wastefulness. I'd throw
away the brittle casing my supermarket
chicken came in instead of, as he did,
meticulously rinsing and recycling it.
I've since heard these kinds of plastic
can't be recouped, and I was thinking now
about whether Wilfrid was right, whether
I should have fought, regardless if the system
was there to receive it, to reuse every
little piece of detritus, to not produce
any in the first place, and the difference
it may or not make, and I remembered
sneaking certain items out into the hall
to push them down the garbage chute at night
just to spare myself the humiliation of
this self-righteous little Frenchman going
through my trash, washing it, and leaving
it to dry in the dish rack, a crystallized
chastisement.

But there was once
he had his whole family over for lunch, it
must have been a Sunday, his son, Theo,
who was my age and a writer, and his two adolescent
daughters, done eating and relaxing with each
other at the table, when I stumbled on
the great pile of their dishes and determined
to be useful. As long as I worked
through it all and disappeared to the canals,
I thought . . . But just as I ran the frayed
sponge over the last bowl, Wilfrid
padded in, energetic as ever, a bit
incredulous though still lacking, I sensed,
the due measure of gratitude. «T'as fait la vaiselle?!»
he said, almost charmed, and, not knowing
how to preserve the dignity of wanting
no credit, I stared dumbly on.

I used to play this game when we were kids too.
Something unexpected would pop into
my head, then I'd retrace for you the sequence
and the stages of how I got from where we were
in Erie to a kitchen in the $19^{\text{ième}}$, from SPAM
to cowabunga, with my friend the zebraman,
who helping was, both then and now, a pleasure.
The trick, the string of scarves crammed
into a thimble. Since we were children, and you
were younger, you marveled
there could be built a bridge at all, and let me
tell you—I was thrilled to entertain you.

A Rift

II

A Rift

Cold Mountain

I stole a cactus from the sacred mountain.
Or was I doing what the mountain asked?
It had been touched with fire once, and
I have a way with plants. I could preserve it.
After all they were both rare
and numerous, on just one ridge. I signed
a contract with the guardian, forgiving him
if I caught hanta and agreeing to
stay within the boundaries. At best
the relationship of what I did to goodness was
ambiguous, like poetry's.

It was a mountain
of white mystics where I spent a week almost
walking into bear prints, fasting, living as
a hermit, though I think we can all admit
a week without a cellphone makes a paltry hermitage.
I bathed in freezing rainwater, ate broth, walked
in circles at a Sufi's grave, watched
the scrub oak mottle and, standing in
a cloud, the sun break on the mesa miles away.
If you need to ask whether something in the cactus
called out for you to take it, it didn't.
On your knees, Pascal says, run your lips over
the prayer, and belief follows . . .

As far as
I can tell it isn't a hallucinogen. That would've been
a bonus. Still its flower tastes delicious,
exquisitely bitter, a very complex bitterness.

They probably aren't considered edible.
It flowers once a year in my window—
a yellow-flecked red nodule with a golden navel.
I sit in the sunroom and remember how
I chanced on the shovel, the stillness
and the theft, the little pulse of sorrow.

Scrub Apostrophe

Juniper shadow where a skittering
whiptail reallocates its heat,
resinous, cool shade littered
with pale-blue seeds, together

we seethe. Then the light we cut into
collapses the dream, and we wake up
asleep, separate again. Shadow caster,
I remember distinctly you seemed like

a friend. Clear as the Jahwist's tree that
burnt without consuming, you
addressed me. "Tell them everything
alive is speaking." More like your outline

since, I've offered absentia like a gift, like
shelter from the elements. Talk about hubris.
Piñon nut in a crown of needles, your polite
flavor drawn from thin air over the banks

of the river, from the riverbed, with a hint of
the swiftness of the water, and the water run
dry, subtly lavenderlike, brings obscure moons
to mind, and a sudden face startles the cliffside.

The Milky Way

Outside actual work is still ripe proof
I've learned.
I've learned. I've learned.
I've learned. Then the night shows I never do.
It circles back to "actual work"—where is it?
In the promise of worth sprouts the probable corn.

I've already attacked the present.
Easy target.
Redeemed, somewhat, considered as fiction.
We inhabit it.
People used to say shit like, "That's so meta."
Now it's, "So you're . . . well, *you*,
teaching a decolonization class at an elite,
private university—do you
feel conflicted?"

Tonight I watched a lithe dog—
half coyote, you insisted—dig
a hole in the square of high desert
you call a yard and, after dark,
craning to look straight up,
I said, "Ah, Osiris's wad."

NEW! CD-R Walkman

"I recently commemorated Rapture—
Sorry, a Raptor—but a birdless Wire
Would have been better." What our Pilgrim
Means Is not inoperable, but it's hard
To understand, especially for a Shovel.
Let's have a good, soft burial, no Frills.
A flashing red Dot on the upper right—

The capital *m* mind retains everything
You don't remember. For about an Hour
After, you're saved, but inaccessible.
Could this—grave-implement—laser a Drive,
Burn the half-deteriorated disk,
And replay your Will, it would be something other
Than rusted Steel metallically cold

To the Task—but you would laugh and be nervous.
If only for your breath. If it weren't such
Trouble escaping, we'd build Buildings out
Of Fields we've moved around in, and we'd walk
Outside insulated, feeding new noises
Directly in our Ears. Only Cicadas
And Ambulances pierce it, but they're

Au-même-temps Hoses that suck and reseal
The Vacuums we've created.

Unknotting

Being *noué comme je*, sweet
companion of early hours, line
between close sisters who catches, like frost on
what's ripened, clear light and cause no
feeling save this severing—save this and you'll
find a lifelong next-to-ness—what's left
the only reel. Save it, too,
and carry it on to
more relatively fruitful meetings, &
to much more relatively fruitful meetings.

Gathering

The smell of laundry wafts from the lilac,
and men of indeterminate gender soften their voices
through the green triangles formed by its branches.
The sky is power lines, colored by the bottoms of trees.

Warmer than the air, the breeze crosses the hills
and enters the cow skull's sockets
on the utmost sides—it has been since before winter.
Going around the lilacs, I see the sources. One notices

I'm standing in the shape of a child, assimilating spring
into my sharp face, my body left in broken sunlight,
and informs another. *What can I steal that isn't already mine?*
my pose asks, belonging to nothing, captured.

Poem

I had an idea. It was like a bat—
a wooden one—and when I swung it
I was on my knees, kneeling
since I was grown. I took it
for granted—that felt good—and then I struck
a match against the dots,
deaf to the elements, until the fire
said,

"Don't freak out. You can't hold
this position long." My coworker, who
maybe doesn't see the same thin
spirit behind the Kubota, controls
it better, gives clear orders, has
purer impulses. Out here the pink
and green atmosphere, the coral
enterprise, messes with our eyes.
The sponge becomes a porcupine.

My head hurts, and I take a crap.
It helps me relax to go outside.

Cowboy

My horns grown here and here,
I was a steer—

all my strength, all my surroundings
stretched out like a grave.

Bright before
a cone of darker values, a whim

burnt out of being—a crushed cedar
sputtered like flame and hung

half-choked before the valley.
Pressed against stone, it

and the somber bar in the space
within it, so long

as air bleeds clear, drew
a little blood.

Between us,
you tasted your own breath.

Into the yellow dusk
streaked with stratospheric violet

clouds we floated, torpedo
and teardrop, over

our legs, above the shrubs. While
you watched

I, most
ember, offset our grazing

into a reaction that couldn't
be touched. We lacked the binocular

exclusive—Everything
at once. Everything at

once. Everything at once—
though apprehending our end

in you almost tilted it into us. Later,
in the cafeteria, we waited

again in their mouths,
and in the defection of violence

to docility
we moved, considered

from the ceiling, in golden
constellations.

Feeding mostly drudgery, without
a hint of the old urge

or its silent concomitant,
you found us again,

cowboy,
in the void of your own resistance.

A Ghost

And so it came to pass, not long after, that it nailed rain.
Both kinds, human and divine.
Living on rice and living on beans and rice,
I can reach into another life.

Ghosts

"Your messages to send, if you're him,
to their names @yahoo.france,
your hand over them waiting to touch and send them—
It's like reaching in the dream . . ."
The footage of the woman sleeping rolls. She's reaching.
"You reach in real life,
but there's only air so you can't grab . . ."

"Oh my," she says. "I think it was a glass!"

"That is its whole life. Think about that."

He was talking about the ghost, the "phantasm."

"It's what I keep saying. Well, the spirit of the thing,
the spirit of the things I said to her," says the other man.
"And when the hunter comes here and asks,
'What would you be willing to sacrifice?'
Why I'll—well, I will!"

"Mmm," the host says. "You will . . . what?"

"Why—"

"Don't say it, Mike!"

"Why, that I'll—"

"Oh, don't say it!"

"That I'll move. I'll move . . . Why—if we have to."

"That's it," said Bill, killing the volume,
"it's for resale value! Look how clean
everything is, how high the ceilings seem.
That's the question, right? Do people buy the house
after because it's haunted or because it was on TV?"

I said, "We have a—"

"No, ours is smoke," he said.
"Not even. You can tell smoke is . . . is there.
You can't really tell this is there.
That's how you know it's the embodiment
of postcolonial consumer capital—
no supply, no demand, but we're still buying.
We've got this ghost on rent.
We'll sell people the idea of the possibility of escape,
right. The ghost is outside. And what's great is
it's already right there, the escape,
in their money. Literally inside the money.
Just buying feels great.
You're a unit of its exchange. And that's freeing.
But right then, after you've bought the thing,
you're unhappy again. Why?
You've bought something you don't need.
You're burdened. What do you do with this thing?
You can't throw it away—that would be wasteful!
Even if you bought an idea, you've got to hold on to it.
And what's more, getting rid of it would be a decision,
and that's just the thing we've been trying to get
away from—"

"How many takes," I said, "do you think it took?"

"To get this actor to seize even half-convincingly?"

"Before it attacked her."

"That's not even her!" said Bill.

"Ours is better," I said. "Do you remember
What Christine used to say?"

"Sure, she'd say
you only ever see it in the kitchen.
Yeah, no, no one's ever seen it anywhere but the kitchen,
and you recognize this catch
like click, click, click, click, air
at the line, you know, where the space changes
like you've got to acknowledge it before you enter.
But Christine would be like,
'Don't you think, sometimes, that it's only ever this,
only exactly this?' I guess she meant banality,
or some harmless lack of evidence,
the condition that should you want to
you could so easily explain away—
a grieving widow sees her husband standing in the snow,
the rest of us only see her grief.
Her grief explains the ghost.
We only see you responding to your own life's scale
and not the explanation, no kind of truth but an alternate,
only the thing, we tell ourselves, you can't see.
You change. Fine. Good. And you see what you were, vaguely,
but what is it that you can't see? That's a koan, friend.
Your lucky number's 12."

"But you don't even believe in it?" I said.

"Is it late at night?" he said. "Am I alone?"

"Yes," I said. "It's very late."

"Am I alone?"

"You're not alone."

"Am I alone?"

"No. You're not alone."

"Hello?"

"Haha," I said.

"Maybe somewhere, if I'm coming home from somewhere
where there were a lot of people and all the lights
are on and the blinds are up so you see light
in the windows and nothing outside except red flashers
in the distance and there's a window open,
so I go back there and it gets inside me, and I seize."

"When it gets inside you?"

"When it gets inside me."

"You guys are trying to make fun of me,"
said Marie, trembling up, almost in tears.

I'd forgotten her.

"You're crying?" Bill said. "Oh shit.
I mean to it—"

"I don't need this,"
she said. Her hair was perfect, pulled tight back
into a perfect bun, and she had on a gray dress
with sparks in it. "There's no need.
I'm not crying." But her tears were huge now,
one from each corner of the left eye rolling unevenly,
one starting fat from the inside corner of the right.
"The two of you," she said. "The two of you
are already . . . are dead already."

I felt disgusted with our conversation,
for having upset her, and maybe for conversation in general,
but I was still curious about it all
and how her insistence on this presence, this inactive being—
"It's active!" she said once. "It combed the ends of my hair."—
well, in truth, I never carried the thought even so far.

"Mark," she said, turning to me. "I'll put a little life
in you just so you can know.
I want you to know what it's like. Only you.
I'll whisper it to you," she said, and she approached,
took her middle finger, wiped the fat, right tear.
Then she wet my ear.

Effortlessness

III

Effortlessness

Underpass

Coming over it for once, seeing it from above,
coming to this spot and seeing Route 20 bend.
13′8″ plus the unknown height of the train carriage, plus my own
height—I had already been fighting the cabin light to see.
I was close. The closed Tae Kwon Do house,
the island between these three roads, the yield sign, flagpole, billboards,
the landscaped embankments—

it's nameless. We're coming to it, a turquoise trapezoid
cut through the hill. I took you here, not specifically.
We passed, blinking, through both of them . . . Anyway,
I went countless, with you and others, to get to the lake.
The lake is proof.   And a train rips into sight
just before we dip beneath its quarter mile of cars. Simultaneity.
Simultaneity. Then the bridge erases a second of rain.

Love Language

New company started it. Only
in the afternoons when he
had us, he explained why they
were with him. He wasn't
flaunting, but living openly, and mom's
thinness—we should ask her—had
nothing to do with him. So we did.
Looking back, it's clear what
she wanted to say.

Determinant
as these things seemed while we
watched their hair and skin shine
through the divide, they were more
like cinder blocks than gophers.
Whether we built pools or bank
branches—should we want to
undermine it? Overcoming,
recreating, and overcoming each
time, we had the rest of our lives.

Upstate

In the middle of white creation, a pond,
yardpiece, worth a swim
and miraculously clear.

You could acknowledge me here.

Brain deep, startling out the fibers,
I had a dream in the water
of projecting glass boxes while
in real life
you birthed a breathing LEGO.

"I'm not cold."

This was our social world.
Goat born without a nose,
a nice gemstone. They help more
than now, now.

The water's wet.
One birch in a line of maples.
Wooden bucket, metal bucket,
tumbled in mischief.

We send them down.

Chinatown

The winter we lived above Nam
Bac Hang, the plastic
like air from an empty squirt gun
pushed our faces. "Blurp blurp,"
said the wedding cake in the
Frigidaire. How many rounds
of ping-pong
did it take before your sister
lost her mind? "His butt
is not that wide!"
And the lease ran out.
Hush pups and clementines
dream-dotted like fireflies
in a township field
the strange grocers.
That's neat! was the refrain
while the old tower watched
unregretted
your Camry disappear on Princeton St.,
and you left tracing a seam
of the shared world, alone.

Edible Arrangement

The deep sexual taste of figs
and the pear's nuptial profundeur
align today like undiscovered planets
secretly influencing this sacred affair.

The one fruit always ripe, the other
almost never—
his eyes perpetually dancing, hers
frozen in wonder.

Charged to read, not to explain
why these angels
appear as foods we rarely integrate,
I feel compelled against my strength
to account for such truths that,
could they germinate directly in their brains,
some among us, and each of us at times,
would either refuse or fail to understand.

While our eyes, or principles of light,
produce, in contrast, a greater space,
and though it's true each sense incorporates
a shadow of its fellows, these live
in their mouths, before speech, within breath,
and so their knowledge becomes essential.
They form the fundamental ties
that we, witnessing, share power to bind.

What feeds these green and living bonds?
We, by shifting something in ourselves,
root down, attract, almost trick,
and control without controlling.

Through such spells, their rings soon shackle them
less to each other than to us who know,
now that we've been asked, to often think
of them together. We are the ones
who set them in their freedom, into the work
that's just beginning. Sweet to the degree
that it persists—this just beginning.

Not under vigilance, but in attunement
of the kind that assists its own forgetting,
we respond to more than what they've asked.
Because we're asked more
than the question posed,
what we add may yet fit nicely.

It is in fact the life this freedom
that depends on their creating, even unconsciously,
the being of the two of them together
exists almost entirely within, and
even after its sudden autonomous
rebirth as something completely different
shocks them to the core, it will continue to.

So how did they conceive this freedom
from us and from themselves?
And can it really be that we have anything
whatsoever to contribute?

First they tasted, then they listened.

Now, just by accepting it, we give
their freedom back to them with interest.

On TV Elsewhere

Diegetic coincidences stopped us like recorders.
    Who would have guessed
that the straight and narrow, near-perfect conformity
    of gender & want so easily
mistaken for the evil it grows beside would also make
    for a difficult life.

It's a mailman's frame of mind.

They were never happy except when they were too preoccupied
to notice. We absorbed that quickly.
                    Their being imaginary
no impediment to that most exalted state's
    raptures, these fights
    of feeling & finger—where our still
    animate corpses
    finally involved, not sadness,
    but the wood that makes up the arrow—
    aimed past sadness.

We didn't know how we were acting,
and though we tried to fill in the gaps with familiar stories,
that's holy.

Brooklyn Is the City

Henry messages, "Come down to the L.E.S.
I'm rolling with Candace and Skittles, Ange,
who else?" But we stay
to watch Consciousness, the pit bull, scrape
out a taller dog's entrails—amazing how purple
the membranes and the blood of nosebleeds
and how drugs are taken seriously.
When the breaker fails and the music stops and in
a hollowed-out factory no one does anything—
Okay, they read Garfield and David
Graeber, stack VHS jackets, and press together
thinking: a helicopter erupts, a fawn corpse,
an object of scorn because dislocated
from the objective, a uniformity of geography
impervious to miles, an adjective, a Pope Leo
with Sides of Beef, a millionth of a molecule,
a thermometer, a vasectomy. They touch
in darkness and ignore the moaning.
I'm there. It's the morning. Ange combs her hair,
and it sounds like Velcro. I take a cotton ball
from the medicine cabinet. A low vertebra tickles
when I pull the puff apart. I press one half into each ear
and think of Saturn. I watch television. A commercial
for Frost Kitchenware shows a white table
set with white napkins, forks, and plates. A beekeeper
vouches for an all-natural cure for malaise.
With an inner ear I hear my grandmother say
"advertisement" the short *i* way. The universe must
have been created by a superhuman—a super
being, she told me last year on the telephone
when I called to talk plans for the winter.
"I know, Grandma," I said. "I know."

On Earth

When we see them
    silhouetted into wire
or flat without the portals
    of our dungeons,
the introspective phase of
    our existence will end.
That we should be gods
    by being first their food
we reject as shallow fate
    though they thrust
worse on us with this
    colder recognition. "We
are being excluded," Edgar says.
    "That's how you can not
believe in them." There was
    in my mind no logical
connection, no cancer,
    at least for now, but I
was searching for the same
    in other language, a
transport to the world
    between the world that
they've found. "Having
    been there recently myself,"
he said, "you should know our
    lives might've been different,
that we plucked these forms
    from liquid air, thinking
we were choosing
    some kind of condiment."

The Gatekeepers

The ape-men came for the manna, but
    it turned to ash in their mouths.
To taste our bread one must move
    farther from want than their measures.
So we cornered them in the pampas
    and trapped them in our computers.
As they war, seek pleasure, and breed, we study
    the information. Now, the data say,
we may soon know why we made them. By eons
    our acts precede whatever use
is served the machine by the bubbles
    expressed in the grease—the love
and fear and loneliness, the longing,
    freedom, and peace—that make
their lot memorable
    whether they earn the future or not.

Speedway Creamer

Take it to the bathroom and
put it in your pocket. Come back
and pay for it. What about some
butter? Your conscience
likes the stimulus. It saddles
your fib in velvet,
breaks it. Now you squirm
when you sit. Supernatural
stillness buried in your
laughter, discoordinated
gestures, you switch off
every fan in the earthship and
drive to the throbbing core, back
to the labor ward. A woman, *non
compos*, clutches at
your ear as you press
her ruptured uterus. Has she
come down from the meth? Can
she consent? Your stitching draws
a compliment—"At least
you're consistent"—from a
resident. "Fucking
sidewalk people," says the
woman's father. "Sure as hell
ain't living with me." At the
back of your mind where
your spirit hangs down like
a uvula, you
swallow him alive. Maybe
that's why when you're

waking up at 3:00—all you can think
    is, "I need coffee and a dick
in me." The cretin that
    becomes us when we titter
at the homeless lunging
    for the car or crushing
industrial caulk into the street, that
    giddy feeling of
absurdity and sorrow, is what
    guides you to the
suffering. You're like a
    dowser's rod jerking
to an underwater
    stream. *What's*
the point of this? you
    think. Break down crying. Four
hours later, purple as
    a bishop's robes and light
as fluorescence, the baby's
    in your hands. You lay her
on her mother's chest. A noise
    like icicles crashing on a
plastic drum catches in
    her throat. A moment
of quiet, then the
    attending leaves to check her
messages. The placenta
    almost radiates as the scrub
nurse eases it into a
    gleaming, clear container.

Punishment Bag

We had been talking in diagrams—
the Villon blueprints superimposed on
"I feel so strongly I couldn't stand up
for myself," but this is different.
To come at it directly from the side,
this is where it hurts. A mouth after
that hastily drawn arrow, you see
a right-sided flicker of dots. It's better
to disbelieve. Not always. Not never.

Punishment Bag

Rosa would wait for me at the station—
"pink umbrella, closed (or open)"—
and I'd settle into life at the Walls,
Les Mureaux, Parisian exurb,
a 90% North African ghetto where
I'd model English at the aptly named
Lycée François Villon and, in my free time,
memorize the medieval ironist's verses, thrilled
to understand when he described, for instance,
a winter so brutal that the wolves
fed on the wind. The school lay
on the other side of a Seuss-like park.
Loraxian trees lined overcultivated walks,
and to the north from squat smokestacks
untold picturesque pollutants billowed
constantly across the open fields where,
I'd been warned, the previous language
assistant used periodically to get fleeced.
The omnipresent "get"—the first
verb I noticed that always required
a more precise transliteration.
Whether to receive, befall, or fetch,
we put it "in tutte le salse," Rosa said.
Petite and commanding, my superior
allowed herself precisely one cigarette per
lunch. On first arriving from Tuscany, she'd spent
weeks on end with her head wedged
in vinyl clamshells at the terminals
of the BnF—the only library I know
with an archival forest—repeating key
expressions like "N'importe quoi" and

"Les fuyards montent le fleuve," distracted
by the Nouvelle Heloïse within, kicking her ribs.
She told me all this in a sub-zero apartment
in Verneuil sur Seine, standing at the range, sliding
the pinkest entrecote I'll ever see around
a pan of electrically heated grease, pining
for a lost astronomer who cared "more
about the stars than me."

Don't think for a second I was diligent
when I say I discovered the plan
for the compelling "pedagogical instrument"
from which this poem derives its title
in the secondary ELS literature. It was the only
good idea in the slim, free pamphlet
my thirty-second Google search for training
yielded me. I'd been assigned ten sections.
Each of the regular English classes across
four levels was required to join me twice
a week for native conversation. Blessedly,
a quarter never came. I mean that I went
to the assigned rooms for an entire year
and sat at the front desk wondering how
many nanograms of gold were buried
in the unnecessarily sleek machine that screened
me from the empty seats while somewhere
in the labyrinthine complex the truants
wandered undetected. Flashing in a blank
Word document, the caret marked 36-
hundred seconds, then I'd stand up
and leave. Either the regular faculty failed

to inform them, or, more likely, after
the first missed class the kids and I made
a tacit pact: They did not want to meet.
I was terrified to teach. They'd smoke clopes
out back, and I'd write (in theory) the poems
that would make my reputation. I might've told
someone the first month, fixed it, corralled
the missing sections. After that, the embarrassment
of a confession would have killed me. Between
empty meetings I'd duck away to the boiler
room housing the industrial washer where, almost
daily, I did my meager laundry, and I'd sit huddled
with my legs crossed, mortally anxious
I'd have to engage the custodial staff
in my remedial French, praying
they'd spare me the necessity.

As for the rest, a few enterprising pupils, God
bless them, wanted to learn English. That's why
it pained me, through the early months, that
an interchangeable procession of 16-year-old
standups with names like Guy, Rachid,
and Maurice spouted off incessantly
in an argot-dense vernacular as beautiful
as it was unintelligible to me. They practiced
their impromptu insult comedy at my expense,
and who could blame them? I once
while relocating to escape an extensive blood-tinted
ceiling leak referred to the affected classroom
as "la chambre"—the bedroom—and repeatedly
insisted that I had just visited Rosa's ass—

my mispronunciation of "Rosa's class"—
to their immense adolescent glee. I lived,
it's worth noting, gratis, in an uninsulated
rector-set apartment behind the school, across
the hall from the school chef, who I along
with everyone found in public the sweetest
man imaginable but whose frequent, sometimes
frightening domestic disputes soon sharpened
my ear to the 9th- and 10th-graders'
comparably extracurricular vocabulary.

Two groundskeepers, early on, assembled
me a bedframe, a box-slat affair unheard of here
in the States and, for all I know, uncommon
there also because, in their confusion, the workmen
clipped the strap securing the slats
to the head and baseboard. Now
through the night the teak panels supporting
the wafer-thin mattress inched together until
inevitably, just before sunrise, my feet crashed
into the open pulpwood structure. By late
October, in the early hours, my breath fogged
in the lamplight and, though I complained
of the broken radiators to the principal, fixes
at François Villon came only "grâce au système D."
I slept in sweats and, when I woke, did sit-ups
to keep warm. I'd gotten practice from the evening
calisthenics that the lithe futch gym teacher
held weekly for the aging faculty, and, so impressed
was I with her tendency to bound down
the school steps two at once with a "Hup, hup,

hup, hup," that I began imitating her on my Escherian
descents into the Paris metro. I might have passed
the whole winter in constant motion if it weren't
that, come mid-November, the giant Auchan across
the park stocked a row of 25€ space heaters. I toted
one home over the vacant pathways, humming
Rimbaud, picturing the blue nights of summer.

I like to pretend the bag the heater came in
is the bag that became it, because soon after
I gathered up the miscellaneous items
propping up or expelled from my mean
existence—a pocket calculator missing
its back shell, an orphaned rook, cheap
aviators, two miniature plush koalas—the idea
was to keep a constantly cycling assortment
of texturally and contextually distinct objects ready
to hand so that the subjected troublemakers
never twice withdrew the same fetish. Here's
how it worked: I filled a black plastic
grocery sack, the punishment bag, with refuse
and trinkets, and when my charges spoke
other than English I instructed them
to remain seated while I held the bag
above their head. They were to reach in
almost to the elbow and, without naming it,
describe whatever their hand grasped. "It's zoft
and made of cloth. You wear it . . . on your foot."
Only when the class identified the thing could
the subject pull the sock out for all to see. "This time,"
I'd say, "the sock is *clean*. Push your luck,

and next time it will be *dirty*." It's possible
I stretched this joke too far when one particularly
prim and guarded junior selected a cardboard
tube with a few dangling scraps of toilet sheet.
Needless to say, the method backfired. They
clamored for more. A few enterprising
polyglots even deliberately regressed
to secure their opportunity.

"It is 'ard. It is 'airy. It grows on ze tree."
Half palm himself, a slender boy named Toni drew
the coconut. "Oh my God. Can I keep it for ma mère?
She uses zis for une soupe délicieuse."
Did any expect, I wonder, that their future
punishments might also take this shape?
"As, barring perhaps the ultimate," I wrote in
an early draft, "our punishments tend to be,
their punishment would be discovery." But
I've come to suspect death won't be different.
Each death, a lot whittled by the life
encasing it, sits until the moment when, keen
or obtunded, conscious or asleep, what's
left of our sense engulfs it, so that our
last living act is learning. Some are spiked like durian
and rupture at their testing, but all, whether
slick and metallic or softly downed, sap
our last heat. With poems, since we're now
explicit, I've often felt similar, like I was reaching
into a bag of mystical geodes, alien
organs, even living entities, angels
or shades whose subglottic existence

it fell on me to translate. To the elbow
and past it I've plunged my arm into
this insubstantial purse. Less than air, its
immateriality flickers like tones of fuchsia
in the smooth interior of certain oysters.
It obscures and aggregates the extradimensional
socks and coconuts that shred the net
of English. But as to who has summoned me
and to what end and for which of my trespasses
or faults, I cannot pretend to answer.

Love

If you forget your friends, even if you forget them all
And insult poets—
God forgives that. But hold out some hope
For lovers and their strange minds.

Because, honestly, is there life anywhere else
Now that fake Virtue rules everything?
Whatever we believed in wandered off, whistling
Like a god, and left us here.

Still, however barren the year proves,
Almost at the right time, from under the snow,
A greenness—the fresh grass—sprouts up,
And sometimes a bird sings

While the woods slowly expand and streams move—
At midday, the breeze is already warm—
Then finally the right moment comes
For a sign of the better times

We still believe in, where something that's enough in itself,
Pure and clear, out of a shining, copper
Ground, can grow—Love,
Incomprehensible, a gift from God.

Some rift in reality lets this one plant
Scatter its seeds from heaven, and it's kept
Alive by invisible nectars and the effortlessness
That radiates out of work's core.

Let it spread into a whole field, a thinking, feeling stretch
Of full-flowered world. And the words we share in love
Will be the language there—here—even now,
Where we carry like the sound of laughter.

punishment bag

Notes

It may come as a surprise to those familiar with my recent ambulance work that I wrote the poem "Quick Recovery" (4) about a year before I'd considered the possibility of a career in emergency medicine. I'd just crested the hill with my doctoral dissertation. A task that had seemed impossible for the better part of six years now seemed to be progressing of its own accord—I could write poems again. Some months or maybe even years before, I'd read a few pieces by Philip Levine, most notably "Fear and Fame," the opener for the collection *What Work Is* (1991). I can't say what brought it to mind, but after so much time engaged in the fluff work of graduate school, I thought I'd better switch tacks and write about the hardest job I could imagine in a voice not my own—a persona poem, why not? Not for the first time would the terrain I mapped in poetry affect my unwritten life, though perhaps it's a bit disappointing in this case that the poem's prophetic character was so literally fulfilled. One could be tempted to imagine such poems—poems that become, whether directly or not, predictions of our future lives—like taproots that penetrate the hidden aquifer where pool our essential selves. I tend to think in my case it's the opposite, that, in fact, my desires are so blank or eroded that whenever I manage an idea of any substance in writing, I instinctively cling to it and partially remake myself as a result. A wreck and not a well.

Lorine Niedecker inspired the sawtooth structure of this and a few other poems in the collection.

"Your Release" (8) is one of three poems here that takes place in the city where I was born: Erie, Pennsylvania. The others are "Gathering" (33) and "Underpass" (47). Around the time of composition, my closest childhood friend was arraigned for a laundry list of trumped-up felony charges. He fled an officer who approached him for appearing unresponsive in a vehicle that was not his at a state-park overlook known as "Vista 1." According to the affidavit, my friend fled the scene, "aimed his vehicle at [another] officer" who had used his patrol car to block egress, "forcing the officer to jump out of the way." From there, pursued by law-enforcement officials from multiple jurisdictions, he "traveled along West Eighth Street, Saint Clair Avenue, and West 10th Street before turning south onto Potomac Avenue," ultimately crashing through a fence on the north end of the Erie Airport, where he continued circling hopelessly through the grounds until his borrowed SUV got stuck in the mud. It was, I remembered thinking, an accident of his race that he wasn't killed. Maybe it's more accurate to say a societal conspiracy worked to spare him. The question for me as I look back over these poems, requested as I've been to shed light on them, is why it should matter—or should it matter?—that I conceived this and some of the other poems in this collection, abstract as they are, to have unfolded in specific times and places, in relation to real persons undescribed or unnamed. Doesn't this tend to make the poems more difficult—simultaneously open to interpretation and uninterpretable—and is this difficulty introduced arbitrarily, for its own sake, or does it otherwise function as an abnegation of the author's responsibility to be clear and make sense? These are the kinds of questions I ought to outrun.

Very little in "Your Release" or in my initial attempt to explain it is provable. For instance, the Taco Bell from which I imagine purchasing gorditas with my friend is in the Eastway Plaza, not the Kmart Plaza (now the Buffalo Road Plaza). In the fiction of the poem, we might have driven—it was, after all, the sort of thing we did in Erie, where it seemed there was always nothing to do—the half mile from the Eastway Plaza to the Kmart Plaza, parked our car, and watched customers leaving Kmart as we ate our food. But the Kmart no longer exists. It was likely closed even at the time this poem was written, and its eventual demolition was the subject of numerous local news articles and forum posts in early 2024. I have a distinct memory of drafting this poem, after a run, in a maroon-covered three-subject spiral notebook in the Blackstone Avenue studio where I lived through August of 2018. I remember it as a summer poem, and I recall precisely that I learned the word *caducous*, borrowed from the technical language of botany and referring to organs that easily fall away, as in, "Poppies have caducous sepals that are shed after the bud has opened," from Max Cavitch's study *American Elegy* (2007), one of the first readings I prepared for my doctoral field exam. The problem with this timeline is that my friend wasn't arrested until February of 2019. His struggles with addiction were well-known to me from as early as 2008 or '09, and it wouldn't have been hard to imagine him landing in jail sometime before my father read me the story of his arrest from the *Erie Times*. If this is true, I imagined my friend's arrest, imprisonment, and eventual release, wrote about it in the past tense, and then, a few months later, my friend was actually arrested. Thankfully he was never imprisoned. He pled down the charges to misdemeanors and faced only a few years' probation.

Maybe I ought to say former friend. We haven't spoken now in ten years.

"Firefield 5 × 50" (9) is written in night vision. It addresses the poet Justin Cox.

Stylistically, "Your Property" (11) is indebted to Dora Malech and Andrew Joron. Writing it, I was thinking of my uncle Joey.

I once asked Ed Roberson a question about lyric poems. "I don't call them that," he said. "*You* call them that." Perhaps the problem, then, is with the category rather than the specimen when I say that "M." (15), of the poems in this collection, poses the greatest set of challenges to my own understanding of what lyric poems do. It would be the rare reader indeed who, without an external prompt, could guess the three things I had in mind with the title: 1) the narrator of Marcel Proust's monumental first-person novel, *A la recherche du temps perdu* (1913–1927); 2) Fritz Lang's magnum opus, *M* (1931); and 3) the poet Margaret Ross. Nor did I ever want them to. The poem further alludes to an offstage and only obliquely described photograph taken by the poet/artist Kai Ihns of a Cooper's Hawk (or a small falcon of some kind) that wedged itself into a fence mid-flight and perished. Again, I remember where I first encountered the word "orphrey," in Eric Linsker's collection *La Far* (2014). When the poem says, "chain-link the handsaw's / cold orphrey," it corrupts a dubious scholarly exegesis of the famous line from *Hamlet*, "I can tell a hawk from a handsaw," that suggests a handsaw is not, in fact, a woodworking tool but another kind of hawk-like bird, then the poem imagines the hawk-like bird in Ihns's photograph wearing its destruction (the chain-link fence) like a priest's alb. The title is, on the one hand, algebraic—that which can be substituted and is to be solved—and, on the other, it signifies an incapacity for substitution—the quiddity that arises when we situate ourselves individually as the operator of a language, the "I" that we all watch ourselves use. This is dramatized directly in Proust's first person, and it is pushed to a limit case in Lang's movie when the pedophilic child-murderer, cornered in a bunker by a vigilante mob composed of organized criminals—"*Hier kommst du nicht mehr raus*"—pleads for his lack of culpability on the grounds that it is not he who has committed the murders since he has stood by internally and watched as an inexorable force murdered children through him; besides, were his accusers not, themselves, guilty and therefore beholden to show mercy?

The question of course is how this conglomeration of essentially private allusions and undisclosed lived experience ought to affect a reader's reading experience. One possibility is that these notes illuminate nothing—or, at least, shouldn't illuminate much—about the poems' effects, as they merely detail the author's best guess at how a specific set of linguistic material came to appear in them and not what that material means or how it behaves when excised from the life that enabled it. Generously, one might understand the experiences behind the poems to exert a distant, barely perceptible gravitational force while the poem's unrelated, internal forces occupy the foreground. Or one might see the disclosure of these experiences and associations as something akin to a painter's account of gathering raw materials and painstakingly extracting from them the specific pigments she used to produce her works. Probably there's a fantasy that a forensic literary scholar could examine these linguistic nuggets—a set of poems that I started out by calling "little dinkers"—and extract the life that produced them, the person that I was, what I read, the friends that I had.

Not so long ago, the New Critics cautioned against the idea that lyric poetry is allegorical—that each item in a poem has a secret symbolic significance that can be cracked once you mail in enough box tops to get the right decoder ring. Overlooking that some short poems—and probably more than the poets themselves could admit—really are jibberized transliterations of prosaic real-life occurrences, a trace of allegory inheres everywhere. Any sign might be another sign in disguise. Probably much of the public dissatisfaction with poetry stems from the feeling that it is a private game played by privileged players, where learning the "rules" requires too much buy-in for too little payout. Can we really fault the students who, intuiting the social gulf between the assigned poets and themselves, decide every word in a poem is a different word in disguise? Only, I suppose, for imaging most poets possessed the discipline and consistency necessary to produce coherent allegories. I remember my own flash of insight in a high-school English class when I realized that William Carlos Williams's "red wheelbarrow" symbolized communism. "No. No. No," Ms. Whalen said. "It is *just* an image." Responding to the scarecrow of this objectivist "just an image" argument some years later, Jim Galvin asked, "Then what about the 'so much depends'?" When I finally read *Spring and All* (1923) and saw that this Williams poem was an extracted fragment from a batshit, book-length composition written primarily in prose and perhaps never even intended to be excerpted, I felt still further that old Socratic feeling: "I know nothing." At any rate, if anyone cares to read my poems allegorically, I can't object. I only ask that they extend the same courtesy to these notes. Nothing here either means what it purports to.

The title "Dreyman" (19) comes from a collegiate German textbook containing the model sentence, "*Dreyman liebt sie und ihre Untreue tut ihm unsäglich weh*," which translates roughly to, "Dreyman loves her and her unfaithfulness causes him unspeakable pain." We'd never met this Dreyman, and we'd never hear of him again, yet his plight, so parallel my own as I labored through the genitive, stuck with me. Conscious poetic effects rarely if ever achieve the raw force of dictionary and grammar-book examples, of "found poetry." At least that's what my old friend Helena Zhang thought when she founded a journal on the principle, *A Similar but Different Quality*.

With language learning, I truly feel myself my father's son. I've written of his mechanical genius elsewhere, but not of his aversion to finishing—well, most anything. He would find a boat rusting behind a barn somewhere out near Titusville and spend a year refurbishing it, reconstructing the engine, polishing the dashboard instruments, replacing the cupholders with his own maple carpentry, and then he'd stop work just before the thing was usable. You could take it out on the lake, maybe, but if you put your foot on a particular place near the engine compartment the motor might drop out. He could never leave go the dream. Similarly, just before she left Iowa, my friend Charlene gave me a shoebox of Moleskins with the first few pages X-Actoed out. I had enough neuroses to understand—starting again in one of these would never really be starting fresh. We discussed a book she had out on the table, something I'd read recently and enjoyed. "Yes," she said, "it's amazing. I haven't finished. When I love a book I read up to the very end and I stop. I don't want to lose it. Maybe that's sentimental? I suppose I should get over it." I cast an eye over her half-vacated apartment. A dozen bookmarks protruded from her titles at the last twenty pages.

Near Fremont, Indiana, in Steuben County, an interstate "ATTRACTIONS" sign advertises Wild Winds Buffalo Farm. I'd passed it some thirty times on various misadventures between Iowa and Erie. It was the summer of 2019 when I finally decided to stop, already early evening. "I think he's done for the day," the store clerk said when I asked after a trip to see the herd. She stood behind her arrowheads and assorted bauxites like a public librarian, her glasses rubber-looped on a braided band. "But you can ask him when he gets back. Just be nice." Silver-maned, limping, his mustache long enough to rustle in the wind, the buffalo keeper loaded me into a seated cage behind a tractor and drove me out to the fields—his last tour for the day. This was Three Paws. He was

Metís, he said, ashamed not to speak Michif, and he spun a few yarns for the tour fee. His ex-wife, he said, had had the gift. The old cows would come visit her in her dreams when there was trouble on the farm. "Go fix the fence by the holding lot," she'd tell him in the morning. "A branch crushed it in the storm last night." And he'd trundle down to find things exactly as she'd told him, the old cow standing by. These were my "Lessons from Three Paws" (20).

I knew nothing then of Indigenous life in America. This was years before, through the combined aid of Chicu Reddy, Kim Parko, and Deborah Jackson Taffa, I found myself teaching at the Institute of American Indian Arts. I asked my guide whether there were still tribes active in the area, and he said, "Well, when you say 'active,' that makes me think of who's still holding powwows." He rattled off a half dozen held by the Potawatomi and others within the span of a short drive. "So, yeah," he said, "I'd say they're active."

For "Cold Mountain" (27) and "Speedway Creamer" (57), I am indebted to Paolo and the other residents of the Lama Foundation who together steer this "massive ship" north of Taos. When I copied this poem into the Maqbara journal, I added, a bit sententiously, "Don't be fooled, hermit. Skepticism is just one posture." A copy of Baba Ram Dass's *Be Here Now* (1971)—originally titled *From Bindu to Ojas*—was tucked in the cabin like a Beatles lyric. It is a far wryer, stranger book than I'd supposed.

"The Milky Way" (30) and "Cowboy" (35) wouldn't exist without the generosity of Lynn Xu, Josh Edwards, and Tilley Roccon. I owe them still more for the time in West Texas. It continues paying dividends.

I prefer to think of "A Ghost" (37) and "Ghosts" (38) as one poem in two parts. If it weren't for Chris Schlegel's insistence that I read alongside him during his tour for *Honest James* (2015), I might never have written it. After serious struggle, I put together a reading in the Melwood Screening Room at the now-defunct Pittsburgh Filmmakers. Taylor Grieshober joined us. It remains the iconic reading of my life. Someday I'll tell you about it.

That spring, in the interludes between my three jobs, I worked my way through Plato's dialogues in the virtually unreadable edition produced for the *Great Books of the Western World*. Soon enough, I found myself less engaged by the philosophizing than I was by the off-stage objects and elements the Athenians mention during their talks.

About that same time, I was walking from the Strip through the Hill District down to the main branch of the Carnegie Library in Oakland a few times a week to read small snippets from the on-site-only edition of R. H. Blyth's *Zen in English Literature and Oriental Classics* (1942). Though not composed in dialogue, Blyth's is another beautiful, dialogic book. I still ache to remember how in that lean year, in the extremest loneliness, I sat poring over imaginary conversations.

This "Underpass" (47) is in Harborcreek, Pennsylvania, just southwest of the Iroquois Avenue and Buffalo Road junction.

Rachel Cusk inspired "Love Language" (48). My own parents never divorced.

"Chinatown" (50) was composed with help from Bernadette Mayer.

Callie Garnett and Colm O'Leary inadvertently commissioned "Edible Arrangement" (51). It's an occasional poem, and I was hesitant to include it. Then again, aren't they all occasional?

Chloe Fournier-Hall was a fourth-year medical student on an obstetrical rotation at the University of New Mexico Hospital when I addressed her in "Speedway Creamer" (57). Most of the events in the poem are drawn from experiences she reported then in the green rush of her career.

I never would have written the second version of "Punishment Bag" (60) if Dan Poppick hadn't pushed me. Sometimes the real poem is hidden in the explanation of the thing we call the poem; sometimes it's much farther than that.

While not the most recently composed piece in this collection, "Punishment Bag" is the one that best bridges it to the present. This morning, while walking a new aide through my mother's care routine—doubtful whether, with her weeping, purulent wounds, my mother will even survive until next weekend when the aide returns—I masked up for the smell. As I explained to the aide, I've dealt with much worse in ambulance work, "but when it's your mom, it hits different." I hadn't said anything, wasn't short, and, like I say, my face was covered. Still my mother looked at me and said, "You're grumpy today." And while I didn't feel it, she was right. Is the final ingredient here my own unintended irritability?

You may know that poetry titles from academic presses, much like scholarly studies, undergo a process of peer review. Usually, two anonymous readers judge the submitted manuscript and decide whether it's worth the press's time. One of this book's reviewers wrote, for example, "LES in 'Brooklyn in the City' should be spelled out someplace at the start of the poem as Lower East Side. Also BnF in 'Punishment Bag' as British National Formulary, same deal. And some others. SOME NOTES WILL FOLLOW IN FINAL REVISIONS, RIGHT?"

It seems the reviewer had no trouble determining that Henry's message in "Brooklyn Is the City" (54) was referring to the Lower East Side. As to what drugs he meant by "Candace" and "Skittles"—or whether he was having one over on us for asking what he was holding in the first place—even Ange and I could only guess. Like most poems in the book, this one archives lived material without toppling entirely into autobiography. For instance, I've never attended and would never attend a dog fight. On the other hand, the reviewer must have settled on "British National Formulary" as the referent for the "BnF" (pronounced /bā en ef/) after a cursory Google search. What could be more appropriate given the poem's own contents? Still, most adult French citizens—my intended audience?—would recognize the acronym instantly as the Bibliothèque nationale de France. The "archival forest" mentioned in the subsequent lines is a striking, though unfortunately unphotographable, architectural feature of the BnF's colossal François-Mitterrand campus.

Anyway, isn't it a trip to imagine gravid little Rosa brandishing a quarter-inch headphone jack and plugging up a physical copy of a UK pharmaceutical reference guide? Repeat after me. That'll learn ya French right.

"Love" (67) is a loose translation of Friedrich Hölderlin's "Die Liebe."

Acknowledgments

This book took shape slowly over the course of fifteen years. So many people had a hand in making it that it feels like an error to put one author on the cover. My first thanks goes to Hilda Raz, Elise McHugh, and the University of New Mexico Press's reviewers. I couldn't imagine a more constructive editorial team.

I am grateful also to the editors of the following journals where versions of several of the poems here first appeared: *Annulet*, *Lana Turner*, the *Partisan Hotel*, *River Styx*, the *Taos Journal of Poetry*, the *Washington Square Review*, and the *Yale Review*.

Many teachers also had either a direct or indirect influence over these poems, namely Sister Marianne Perrone, Terry Healey, Bridget Whalen, Paul Cancilla, Marcelle Clements, Matthew Rohrer, Geoffrey Nutter, Jim Galvin, Arda Collins, Mark Levine, Doug Powell, Joyelle McSweeney, and Srikanth "Chicu" Reddy. I've learned the most from Chris Schlegel, Jessica Laser, Dan Poppick, Callie Garnett, Justin Cox, and Kai Ihns. To Jessica Laser I owe special thanks for some last-minute editorial pressure. She found a few pockets of fat where I thought there were none—not that I could always bring myself to trim it. Kai Ihns helped me back to the writing desk when I'd all but given up on poetry. This book wouldn't exist if it weren't for that. Chris, Callie, and Justin have been my most supportive readers. They've probably placed too much faith in my abilities; I hope someday to justify it. Lisa Wells encouraged a narrative strain in my work just as it was emerging, and, from the James Merrill House, Rob Schlegel sorted out a few hiccups in the style.

I need to mention a few other mentors, poets, friends, and kindred spirits who, whether they know it or not, influenced my work here: Angelica Bess, Margaret Ross, Grant Souders, Gena Salorino, Kyle Van Noy, Albert Hall, Devon Dill, Roxane Izadian, Strummer Hoffston, An Duplan, Robert David Carey, Max Maller, Shelley Sota, Ashleigh Cassemere-Stanfield, Caryl Pagel, Sony Ton-Aime, Imani Elizabeth Jackson, Rachel Mannheimer, Maggie Millner, Alicia Wright, Ken Warren, Eric Slauter, Debbie Nelson, Joel Rhone, Noah Hansen, Adam Fales, dg nanouk okpik, and Deborah Jackson Taffa.

Kevin King is a great skeptic and a greater friend. He administered the antivenom. I owe so much to him and Li Jiang.

Love to my parents, Joanne and Craig, and to my siblings, Adam, Kristen, and Florie.

Finally, Chloe, thank you for everything, for believing in me and for enabling me to become the better poet and person this book can't show that I am.